W9-BHI-071

SandCastle

Word Families Set 5

-og as in dog

Amanda Rondeau

Consulting Editor Monica Marx, M.A./Reading Specialist

ABDO
Publishing Company

Published by SandCastle™, an imprint of ABDO Publishing Company, 4940 Viking Drive, Edina, Minnesota 55435.

Printed in the United States.

Credits
Edited by: Pam Price
Curriculum Coordinator: Nancy Tuminelly
Cover and Interior Design and Production: Mighty Media
Photo Credits: Comstock, Digital Vision, Eyewire Images, Hemera, PhotoDisc, Rubberball Productions, Stockbyte

Library of Congress Cataloging-in-Publication Data

Rondeau, Amanda, 1974-
   -Og as in dog / Amanda Rondeau.
     p. cm. -- (Word families. Set V)
   Summary: Introduces, in brief text and illustrations, the use of the letter combination "og" in such words as "dog," "clog," "bog," and "frog."
   ISBN 1-59197-251-5
   1. Readers (Primary) [1. Vocabulary. 2. Reading.] I. Title.

PE1119 .R695 2003
428.1--dc21
                                       2002038227

SandCastle™ books are created by a professional team of educators, reading specialists, and content developers around five essential components that include phonemic awareness, phonics, vocabulary, text comprehension, and fluency. All books are written, reviewed, and leveled for guided reading, early intervention reading, and Accelerated Reader® programs and designed for use in shared, guided, and independent reading and writing activities to support a balanced approach to literacy instruction.

Let Us Know

After reading the book, SandCastle would like you to tell us your stories about reading. What is your favorite page? Was there something hard that you needed help with? Share the ups and downs of learning to read. We want to hear from you! To get posted on the ABDO Publishing Company Web site, send us e-mail at:

sandcastle@abdopub.com

SandCastle Level: Transitional

-og Words

clog

dog

hog

hot dog

jog

log

Rob helped his dad
fix a clog in the pipe.

Kate likes to hold
the dog.

The hog is very dirty.

Larry ate a hot dog at
the picnic.

Cara likes to jog in the morning.

The deck has a log railing.

Hog, Frog, and Bulldog

Hog and Frog took
a walk in the fog.

They met Bulldog,
who was stuck in a bog.

Bulldog said, "Please hand me that log."

"Oh, dear me!" said Hog.

"We'll help you," said Frog.

They rolled the log
into the bog

and pulled out Bulldog.

"Thank you, Hog and Frog!

I'll join you in the fog,"
said Bulldog.

They laughed
and played leapfrog

and then ate ten hot dogs!

The -og Word Family

bog	frog
bulldog	hog
clog	hot dog
cog	jog
dog	leapfrog
fog	log

Glossary

Some of the words in this list may have more than one meaning. The meaning listed here reflects the way the word is used in the book.

bog   land that is wet and spongy

clog   a shoe that often has an open back and a wooden sole; something that blocks something else

fog   water vapor that forms a mist in the air

laugh   to make a sound at something funny

morning   the part of the day before noon

railing   a barrier that is often part of a staircase or deck

About SandCastle™

A professional team of educators, reading specialists, and content developers created the SandCastle™ series to support young readers as they develop reading skills and strategies and increase their general knowledge. The SandCastle™ series has four levels that correspond to early literacy development in young children. The levels are provided to help teachers and parents select the appropriate books for young readers.

Emerging Readers
(no flags)

Beginning Readers
(1 flag)

Transitional Readers
(2 flags)

Fluent Readers
(3 flags)

These levels are meant only as a guide. All levels are subject to change.

To see a complete list of SandCastle™ books and other nonfiction titles from ABDO Publishing Company, visit **www.abdopub.com** or contact us at:

4940 Viking Drive, Edina, Minnesota 55435 • 1-800-800-1312 • fax: 1-952-831-1632